What Is Content Strategy?
A Beginner's Guide To Standing Out Online

A simple plan for developing a content strategy and learning
the basics of how content marketing works

SANDRA SHILLINGTON

What Is Content Strategy?
A Beginner's Guide To Standing Out Online

By

Sandra Shillington

Table of Contents

Chapter **Page**

Introduction

If you're an entrepreneur, blogger or small business you probably don't have millions to spend on a marketing campaign. That's why improving your web presence is so important. Creating your own quality content is a key part of doing just that - and to improving traffic and selling your products. The problem is many people don't have a strategy in place to do this well. They think of topic ideas on the fly. They're always in search of what to write about next. They react to the latest trends in hopes of the next viral idea. Creating unique, quality content consistently can be a daunting task, especially if you're not a marketing expert. What's the solution? Practical, tangible steps to make it easier. You need a formula to follow.

What Is Content Strategy? A Beginner's Guide to Standing Out Online will help you get started. It will be your formula to supercharge your content marketing and to write unique content that works and sells for you. It's your framework to plan and create endless, powerful content for your blog or business. You'll strategically craft your message and never run out of ideas. Even better, you'll have fresh, quality content always ready to go.

While there's no doubt that technology has made us more efficient than ever, you have Google Calendar, iCal and all kinds of ways to sync your data between your phone, computer and tablet. Did you know that putting pen to paper still has its merits? Research shows that handwriting boosts retention and allows us to use the parts of our brain that we don't use when we type on a keyboard. Something happens when we're doodling or brainstorming with a pen in hand. We solve problems. We develop perspective. We enrich our thought process. As we write, we formulate a solution - even though we may not yet be aware of it. It's slower than a keyboard. We're forced to concentrate more. Writing by hand gives us time to think. The act of putting pen to paper in your own handwriting somehow makes your ideas truly your own.

There's something to be said for having one place to track our ideas and our time. You get everything out of your head and stored in one location. That's where the companion planner for this book comes in. It's called *The One-Year Content Strategy Workbook for Entrepreneurs* and it helps you put in place the concepts explained in this book.

But What About Digital?

All that said, maybe you prefer all things digital, and you're not interested in handwriting your plans in a journal planner. If this is you, the system in this book will still work for you. You can use the same concepts to create a digital version of your content strategy. We'll talk more about exactly how to do this as we go along.

How is this book organized?

Everything discussed in this book is organized according to the pages in your planner - each dedicated to a specific subject. You can make this system completely unique to you and your particular goals for your blog, website or business.

This book will walk you through the steps of setting up your own content strategy plan. If you have a blog or business and you're looking to create content to improve your online presence, this book is for you. When you're finished, you'll have all the information you need for long term and short term planning - all at your fingertips with no more sifting through pieces of paper, post-it notes, text messages, emails and computer files.

Chapter 1

Documenting Your Content Strategy

You know you need a strategy for your blog or business, but it's overwhelming to think about everything it takes to put a strategy in place. You may already have many content ideas in mind - ebooks, courses, and blog topics, but they never seem to become a reality. You may feel disorganized, and you don't know what to focus on first. What's most important? According to Hubspot, companies who blog receive 97% more links to their website, and they receive 67% more leads than those who do not. The more you blog, the more traffic you generate over time. While it's clear that blogging is a crucial part of content marketing, it takes planning, resources and effort to make it worthwhile.

This book will help you create a structure for blogging and all those other ideas you have roaming around in your head. It will help you manage your time and prioritize. Once you have a structure in place, you can turn it into repeatable, reliable systems - allowing you to convert browsers to buyers.

According to the Content Marketing Institute, those who have a documented content marketing strategy are more successful and are not as overwhelmed with the tactics of content marketing. Keep in mind there isn't a one-size-fits-all approach to developing your strategy. Your approach will be as unique as you and your business. However, to be successful, you must document your strategy so that you can internalize it and refer to it often. Your content strategy planner can help you do just that.

In many ways, creating a content marketing strategy is as much an art as as it is a process. Putting pen to paper has a way of stimulating creativity that a keyboard and mouse can't accomplish. As mentioned previously, research provides compelling evidence that pen and paper can be useful in goal setting and brainstorming activities because it takes more time and allows the mind to deliberate. In a 2009 study conducted by Bangor University and branding agency Millward Brown, they used MRI imaging to evaluate the effects of digital and paper media on the brain. They concluded that paper involves more emotional processing and produces more brain responses associated with feelings.

Handwriting slows you down and forces you to think and ponder. As writer Lee Rourke explains in an article for The Guardian, "For me, writing longhand is an utterly personal task where the outer world is closed off, just my thoughts and the movement of my hand across the page to keep me company. It's a deep-felt, uninterrupted connection between thought and language which technology seems to short circuit..."

Another benefit of a written planner is you can it with you wherever you go. You can work on it whenever and wherever you want. When a thought or idea comes to mind, you can jot it down. It gets out of your head and onto paper. Writing on a page stays on a page. When you make a change, you cross it out. Writing on a computer can be deleted - with the ideas gone forever, never to be reconsidered. The pace of writing ideas in longhand lends itself to being more thoughtful.

Not a pen to paper kind of person?

All that said, perhaps you'd rather stick to using technology. That's okay. With digital planning apps such as Evernote, Goodnotes or Notability, you can use the concepts in this book to create a digital content plan.

No matter if your journal is handwritten or digital, you can be more intentional about your content writing plan and be inspired to keep moving forward toward your big goals. It will be your roadmap that tells you what you're going to create, and when and how you're going to create it. You'll track your progress and reach new milestones - skyrocketing your business growth along the way.

Chapter 2

The Pages of Your Content Planner

You can use any notebook to create your content planner, or you can purchase the *The One-Year Content Strategy Workbook for Entrepreneurs* and record everything there. Either way, what makes it different from other planners or journals is how it's organized into the following sections:

The Index

The Index is essentially a Table of Contents. You'll reserve the first few pages in your notebook to set this up. Your pages are numbered, and everything in your journal will be indexed here on the first pages of your planner. This will help you easily find your most important information. On your Index, you'll write down the page number and the subject. It's important to index your journal as often as possible. Ideally, you should index anything new as soon as you create it.

The Legend

Next to the Index you'll have a Legend of the symbols you choose to identify each type of entry. For example, you can use boxes to signify tasks, circles for events, triangles for accomplishments and simple bullets for notes. I've included a list what is generally used, but feel free to choose your own based on what is most meaningful to you.

The Planning Logs

Use your notebook to plan and track notes, tasks and upcoming events for long-term, medium-term and short-term planning of your content.

The Collections

If you are an enthusiastic list maker, you'll love using the "Collections" in your content strategy planner. You can create Collections for anything, such as a list of books to read, lists of topics to research, a list of articles you would like to write, and so on. You can create a new Collection for any interest or new topic you may want to add.

Chapter 3

Getting Started

Supplies You'll Need

To assemble your content strategy planner, you can keep things simple or get creative - it's up to you. Your journal is unique to you and your business. You may have sees a lot of highly creative journals out there - the elaborate art, extensive doodling and details can be a little intimidating if you're not feeling that creative. Don't let that discourage you. Your content strategy planning notebook should be useful for you - not anyone else.

Here are the supplies you'll need to get started.

Notebook - Any type of notebook will work, but it should be large enough to create your pages and write in easily, yet small enough to carry with you comfortably. Many people prefer a notebook with blank pages, a light dot grid or graph paper. Keep in mind this will be your content planning bible. You'll be using it all the time and carrying it around with you. If you're not interested in setting up your own journal, you may want to purchase *The One Year Content Strategy Workbook for Entrepreneurs*. This is a pre-designed planner that corresponds to the concepts described in this book. Everything is set-up for you with fill-in-the-blank pages so you can get started with your content planning right away.

Digital App - If you're going to create a digital notebook, visit Evernote, Goodnotes or Notability and set up an account. You'll also want to download the app for your mobile device, so that you can take your digital journal with you wherever you go. You can use the same principles and set up the same Collections described in this book within a digital app such as these.

Pens - Many people like to get creative by decorating and embellishing their pages with felt-tip or artist's pens. Artist pens are more neat and precise than ballpoint pens. They're also more useful for elaborate lettering and decorating if you choose to do that. Different colors will allow you to color code your entries and will make it more interesting and motivating. Popular brands for journaling pens include Faber-Castell, Staedtler and Pilot.

Ruler - Preferably a clear plastic ruler, for keeping your pages neat and drawing graphs/grids etc.

Construction Level - You can use a construction level to keep your lines straight. Simply project the beam on your page and write directly on the straight line.

White-Out Tape - For any corrections you may need to make.

Sticky Tabs - To quickly locate different sections of your planner.

Stickers/Washi Tape - If you'd like to get creative and embellish your pages.

Stencils - If you're not into drawing, stencils allow you to draw headers and other decorations for your pages.

Chapter 4

Setting Up Your Planner

When setting up your planner you'll be creating separate pages for each of your planning logs. If you purchased *The One Year Content Strategy Workbook* everything is already set up for you. If you're setting up a digital journal, you can follow the same steps. You'll create a new digital note to represent each page of your planner.

Step 1 - Number Your Pages

The first thing to do in your blank notebook is number the pages. This will help you keep track of where everything is as you add to the journal.

Step 2 - Create An Index

Next, create an Index at the front of your planner. Each time you add to your journal you'll reference the entry by adding its page number and description to the Index.

Step 3 - Create Your Legend

You can choose your own or use the following example symbols to describe each item:

• Tasks are listed as a bullet point.

X Completed Tasks are crossed off with an X

> Migrated Tasks moved into the future are indicated by an arrow

> Scheduled Tasks are shown by an arrow in the opposite direction

O Events are represented by an open circle

— Notes are signified with a dash

*   High Priority - starred items indicate they are high priority

I   Inspiration - items that are labeled with the letter "I" are for inspiration

NP New Posts - are labeled with the letters "NP"

Tasks include any actionable item, such as "research this topic" or "write an outline." To mark a task as complete, cross off the bullet with an X. To "migrate" tasks that haven't been completed, but need to be completed on a future day, turn the bullet into an arrow, like this: >

Events, represented by open circles, can be things such as "Webinar Training."

Notes, represented by a dash, can be anything you want to remember such as ideas that you come across, thoughts, observations, or points covered in a class or a meeting.

Starred items are High Priority, while items that are labeled with the letter "I" are for Inspiration. New Posts are represented by the letters "NP."

You'll use a combination of these bullet types in your Daily Logs to list anything you need to do, remember or record each day.

For a digital planner, you can set up the legend in the same way using keyboard symbols.

Step 4 - Create Your Planning Logs

When you create your logs, remember to add the page numbers and references to your Index. Planning will be divided into the three following types of logs:

Future Log (Long Term Planning)

Editorial Goals For This Year

When you create content that's closely tied to your goals, everything you do has a purpose. You'll know how each piece of content you write will help you attain your goals.

Mission Statement

To get started you'll want to write your mission statement for the year. What will you seek to accomplish through your content? You'll want to consider your Audience Persona in this statement. We'll discuss creating your Audience Persona in the next chapter.

Break your mission statement down into actionable steps. Determine your goals for each quarter, then determine what content pieces will help you achieve it. For example:

• Increase Facebook group members to 400

• Make $2,000 profit

From there, you can set your actionable steps for the content you need to create:

• Create a new incentive to join the group

• Write a bonus ebook as a thank you gift to those who purchase my product

Each quarter, take a look at your progress and decide on a few more actionable steps to get closer to each goal.

In *The One Year Content Strategy Workbook*, you'll find an area to write a Mission Statement on page 2, on the Editorial Goals For This Year page.

The Year Ahead

This is an at-a-glance look at your entire year. This doesn't need to be very in-depth. It's simply a place to record future events that you need to remember, and/or long-term goals you want to achieve.

The easiest way to create your Future Log is to divide it into two double-page spreads with six equal sections each. Label them with the 12 months of the year. Use each section to note important things happening that month.

In *The One Year Content Strategy Workbook*, you'll find the Year-At-A-Glance on page 18, immediately before the Monthly Planning logs.

Monthly Log (Medium Term Planning)

Editorial Plan For The Month

Your first page for your monthly log will highlight your Editorial Plan for the month. You'll title the top of the page with the name of the month, such as "January Editorial Plan." You can list things like events and milestones for an at-a-glance look at the month. We'll get into the specifics of planning out your Editorial Calendar in Chapter 6

Editorial Plan By Week

Each Monthly Editorial Plan page is broken down into four weeks. Here you'll write down all the things that you'll need to complete each week during that month. Obviously you won't be able to foresee certain tasks, but it's a good place to make a list of everything you can think of at the beginning of each month.

In *The One Year Content Strategy Workbook*, you'll find Monthly Editorial Plan pages starting on page 19, immediately after the Year-At-A-Glance page.

Daily Planning Log (Short Term Planning)

Editorial Plan By Day

The Daily Log is the foundation of the planner. It's your daily To Do List. Don't worry about planning out the Daily Logs in advance. You'll simply fill them out as you go. Each day you'll write down the date and list the tasks and events of that day. Throughout the day you can jot down any thoughts, ideas or note anything else that comes up. At the end of the day, you can migrate your new notes to any relevant checklist or other area of the journal. If you have any open tasks that you didn't complete, you can migrate them to the next day or to another day.

Your first step of each day is to write in your Daily Log. You'll look at your unchecked tasks and write down the things you need to do that day. Check your "Monthly Editorial Plan" and "Editorial Plan By Week" to make sure you're in alignment with your content plan. Write down the items and events of the day. During the day you can check off tasks as you accomplish them and write down notes as you move through your day. To start your first Daily Log, enter the date and begin bullet listing your tasks for that day, using the Legend you created in Step 3.

In *The One Year Content Strategy Workbook*, you'll find the Daily Log pages starting on page 20, immediately after the Monthly Editorial Plan page for January.

Step 5 - Create Collections For Content Writing

This is where your content planner becomes unique to your business and helps you plan your content. The different sections will help you gather notes, ideas and lists on a specific topic, and they help you manage ongoing projects. You'll use the pages to organize each aspect of content writing and planning a strategy to create client attracting content for your blog or business.

Chapter 5

Collections for Your Planner

Your Collections will help you plan your content strategy and guide you to a specific plan of action for your blog or business. They will provide a way for you to keep all of this important information in one place. We'll now turn our attention to the recommended Collections for your planner. These specific Collections will help you clearly define important aspects of your business and will help guide other important decisions as you expand your plan.

Here are the recommended Content Writing Collections:

• Your Brand Identity

• What is your purpose or promise?

• What makes you unique?

• What do you stand for?

• How are all the above communicated?

• Who are your primary competitors?

• How do they talk and present themselves?

In , you'll find the "Brand Identity" collection on page 3, immediately after "Editorial Goals For This Year."

Target Market/Audience Persona

Who is going to see the content you create? The best content is designed to answer the most pressing pain points of your target audience. You must have empathy for them and understand their situation.

You'll want to start with the things you can measure such as age, gender, location, job title, etc. Then you'll want to define other attributes you can't measure such as attitudes, belief systems, values or interests. You may ask yourself questions such as:

- What's important to them?

- What sources do they trust?

- What values matter to them?

- How do your competitors tap into the same market?

- What are their reading habits?

- What do they need or want?

- What do they need help with?

- What motivates them?

- What are they searching for online?

- What do they like?

- Where do they look for it?

In *The One Year Content Strategy Workbook*, you'll find the "Target Market" collection on page 4, immediately after "Brand Identity."

From there, you'll develop your Audience Persona, which is a general representation of your ideal customer. A well crafted persona is a key component of your strategy. Think of it as a composite sketch of an individual person. This helps you visualize to whom you're targeting your message. You may also want to include a picture of this fictional character using stock photography to solidify your vision of this person.

Give this person a name and write a story about this person. Describe this person's traits. Describe his/her environment, feelings and daily activities. How will this person find your content? How does this person usually find answers to problems? Do they search on Google? Do they use community sites such as Quora or Reddit? Are they Facebook users? Pinterest users?

Having a buyer persona helps you understand what kind of content you should be writing to attract your target customers. By taking the time to clearly write out your persona, you have a consistent guide for everyone who creates content for your business. You can write specifically to that audience and make sure all of your content aligns with the solutions they're looking for or the problems they're trying to solve. It provides a snapshot of who your buyers are and helps you communicate with them on their own terms.

In *The One Year Content Strategy Workbook*, you'll find the "Target Market" collection on page 5, immediately after "Target Market."

Content Style Guide

Consistency and brand messaging can suffer if you don't have guidelines in place. A Content Style Guide is a set of content rules that keeps everyone who works on your content in the same voice. It helps establish your brand identity that your customers will grow to know and trust. It covers image, identity, grammar, language, formatting and tone. Your style guide will:

• Keep your tone, voice, and messaging consistent

• Guide your team on how to write for your audiences

• Help maintain a recognized quality and brand identity

• Convey the essence of your brand

• Result in more effective content

What are your standard fonts? What are your colors? Do you end your posts or emails in a certain way? What is your desired tone and voice? Pick three attributes that describe your brand. Professional yet friendly? Humorous? Irreverent? Edgy? Quirky? Warm? Traditional? Sophisticated? Modern? Classic? Serious? Masculine? Feminine? Natural? In upcoming pages, we'll be discussing your Brainstorming spreads in your journal to create your brand voice. Once you've arrived at the three most descriptive attributes, you can write them on your Content Style Guide page.

The words, tone and style you use in your writing convey what your brand is all about. It should be consistent across all of your content - social media posts, emails, advertising, packaging and so on. By taking the time to define this in your Content Writer's Bullet Journal, you solidify your voice and tone. It prevents you from having a random combination of voices across all of your platforms. It helps you create a consistent image of your brand and makes sure you stick with your brand voice. Even more important, it keeps you from sounding like everyone else. Your Content Writer's Bullet Journal helps you curate your unique brand.

In *The One Year Content Strategy Workbook*, you'll find the "Content Style Guide" collection on page 6, immediately after "Audience Persona."

List of Keywords

You'll need to optimize your content for search engines to rank for the right keywords to drive relevant traffic to your website. A few tools to help you with keyword research include Ubersuggest and Keyword Tool. List all of the keywords you've identified so you have them in one location to easily refer to.

In *The One Year Content Strategy Workbook*, you'll find the "List of Keywords" collection on page 7, immediately after "Content Style Guide."

List of Power Words

Power words instantly grab the reader's attention by skillfully evoking emotion. By using them strategically in your content, you hook the reader's attention. You'll find several lists of Power Words in the resource section at the end of this book. Keep a list in your journal of the words that resonate with your brand and refer to them regularly.

In *The One Year Content Strategy Workbook*, you'll find the "List of Power Words" collection on page 8, immediately after "List of Keywords."

Lead Magnets

What giveaways or promotions will you use for opt-ins? Keep track of them here and for what purpose you'll be using them.

In *The One Year Content Strategy Workbook*, you'll find the "Lead Magnets" collection on page 9, immediately after "List of Power Words."

Published Content List

A list of all of your published content in one place helps to schedule social sharing and know where to link from for new pieces of content and new posts. It provides an overview of all your content so you know what topics you can add to your content strategy. Make sure to include keywords that go with each piece of content to make it easy to reference back to them later. You can use this list when you want to interlink to any of your older content that is still relevant. When doing this make sure your content is current and determine if you need to update any of your existing content.

In *The One Year Content Strategy Workbook*, you'll find the "Published Content" collection on page 10, immediately after "Lead Magnets."

Your Promotional Channels

Once your content is published, it's time to get busy promoting it. While there are many ways to promote your content, some will work better for you than others. It depends on your type of business and your content. Create a page in your journal to record and keep track of how well your channels are performing. You can't be all things to all people, so you'll want to determine which promotional channels work best for you. List these channels in your journal:

Social Media - List your social media accounts. What platforms are your biggest traffic source?

Outreach - When you link to others in your blog posts, most people won't hesitate to share your post with their audience - thus increasing your credibility in the eyes of Google. That's why it's important to always contact them every time. Send an email to anyone you mention in your content.

Email - Send an email to your list of subscribers about your latest content.

Paid Promotion - Most social media platforms offer the option to run sponsored posts.

In *The One Year Content Strategy Workbook*, you'll find the "Promotional Channels" collection on page 11, immediately after "Published Content."

Brainstorm

By brainstorming topics your audience is interested in, you can come up with specific topics and keywords to use as the foundation for all of your content. You can also brainstorm ideas for new products, collaborations and social media ideas. It can be away for you to organize your mind, especially when you have a lot of ideas flowing.

You can start your brainstorm by answering these questions:

- How can you provide what your audience is searching for?

- How does your business match up with the needs of your target audience?

- How are you different?

- How can you deliver the answers or solutions to your audience? Is it through blog posts, courses, email newsletters, ebooks? Write down every method you can think of to deliver your message. Remember, you can provide the same content in multiple formats.

- What kinds of problems do you solve?

Also brainstorm ideas to define the voice of your blog or business. Write down as many adjectives you can think of that describe your brand. Is it quirky? Encouraging? Friendly? Sassy? Professional? Fun? Irreverent? Knowledgeable? This will help you more clearly define your voice for your Content Style Guide we discussed earlier.

One way to brainstorm is to use a mind-map, which is a visual tool used to represent the different parts of a given topic. For example, you could use a mind-map to brainstorm themes to cover in your blog. Another form of brainstorming is called the "brain dump," where you set aside an uninterrupted period of time to jot down all the ideas that come to mind. Write down as many ideas and topics you can think of that your audience might be interested in.

Ask people who interact directly with your audience for their input, such as customer service reps or sales reps. Plug those words into Google's Keyword Planner or Merchant Words and see what comes up. Finally, ask family or friends what they think or feel about your website or blog. If their impressions don't line up with the adjectives you have in mind, then you know you need to improve your message to make it more clear.

Remember, a confused mind will not buy from you. That's why you must clearly and succinctly convey your message. The moment your audience is confused, something else will grab their attention, and they're gone. To build the necessary trust, your audience must understand exactly what you do and how it will help solve their problem.

In *The One Year Content Strategy Workbook*, you'll find the "Brainstorm" collection on pages 12-13, immediately after "Promotional Channels."

Content Ideas

For your content to be successful, you need to remain strategic in what you're creating and avoid the trap of reacting to the latest hot topic or trend. You want your content to be directly related to your business goals. The key to never running out of content ideas is having a repeatable system to follow for generating ideas. Great content writers have a process which they rely on to consistently produce high-quality content ideas. Sometimes ideas aren't always apparent. They take some time and creativity to develop. You can use your planner to provide a framework to research and uncover ideas. It will also help you develop a predictable flow of original ideas.

This section in your journal helps you do just that. It helps you complete your editorial calendar and plan out your content in advance. With an ongoing notebook of ideas for each type of content, you can quickly reference ideas for each area of your content. Because you're coming up with many content ideas at once, you'll be able to group together similar tasks when planning your editorial calendar.

From your brainstorm list, break your ideas into similar groups. What makes sense to your business goals? Based on your keyword research of estimated search volume, difficulty and opportunity, assign a priority to each word or topic.

Determine which ones will best serve your goals and the needs of your audience. Make sure everything aligns with your brand voice and the needs of your customer persona.

You may decide to create a separate journal for each type of content you plan on creating. For example, you may want to create an individual notebook for:

- Blog Post Ideas/Categories

- YouTube/Video Ideas

- Ebook Ideas

- Emails

- Courses

- Podcasts

We'll discuss more on developing your ideas in Chapter 7 when we explore different types of content for different purposes.

In *The One Year Content Strategy Workbook*, you'll find the "Content Ideas" collection on page 14, immediately after "Brainstorm."

Swipe File

A Swipe File is a place to hold ideas that inspire you. When you come across an article, website, or picture that is interesting to you or aligns with your mission, save it to your swipe file. You can keep a written list in your planner of inspiring websites. Your Swipe File may also be a physical folder, or a digital folder where you store these ideas. You'll refer to your Swipe File when you're looking for ideas and inspiration.

In *The One Year Content Strategy Workbook*, you'll find the "Swipe File" collection on page 15, immediately after "Content Ideas."

Inspirational Quotes

Create a page for inspirational quotes that you want to remember or refer to later.

In *The One Year Content Strategy Workbook*, you'll find the "Inspirational Quotes" collection on page 16, immediately after "Swipe File."

Books To Read

Include a list of books that would be helpful for content research and gathering ideas.

In *The One Year Content Strategy Workbook*, you'll find the "Books To Read" collection on page 17, immediately after "Inspirational Quotes."

Notes

A place to keep notes is essential. Whether it's about a specific project, meeting notes, or research notes about a content strategy, being able to keep your notes all together for reference is crucial. Do you struggle with time management?

Your Notes can help you accomplish more writing by reducing the time you spend on non-writing activity during your writing time. They can be springboards or specific starting points for your daily, nightly or weekly writing time.

For example, you could include editorial notes when editing an eBook, or write down questions that you think the audience may be asking. For example:

Introduction > Needs a better title.

Question for Chapter 2 > Why does the reader care about this?

In *The One Year Content Strategy Workbook*, you'll find the "Notes" collection toward the back of the planner, starting on page 199, immediately after the Daily Logs.

Lists of Resources

Keep track of websites that offer quality stock images, your affiliates, places to submit blog posts, websites that pay for guest posts, and other resources. Customize it to include whatever tools and resources you use.

In *The One Year Content Strategy Workbook*, you'll find the "List of Resources" collection toward the back of the planner, starting on page 205, immediately after "Notes."

List of Competitors

It's helpful to pay attention to what your competitors are doing so you know how to differentiate yourself. Keep a list of who stands out in your niche and check your performance against theirs.

In *The One Year Content Strategy Workbook*, you'll find the "List of Competitors" collection toward the back of the planner, starting on page 206, immediately after "List of Resources."

List of Outbound Links

Include external content sources and influencers that relate to your content. Link them to your blog posts, articles, ebooks and training content as authoritative resources.

In *The One Year Content Strategy Workbook*, you'll find the "List of Outbound Links" collection toward the back of the planner, starting on page 207, immediately after "List of Competitors."

Contacts List

This is to keep track of companies and contacts for cross collaborations.

In *The One Year Content Strategy Workbook*, you'll find the "Contacts List" collection toward the back of the planner, starting on page 208, immediately after "List of Outbound Links."

Chapter 6

Planning Your Editorial Calendar

Your Editorial Calendar will live within your Monthly Log that we set up in Chapter 4. It will give you a visual picture of how your content plan lays out. It will also keep you on track and help you identify if you need to add anything, or if you have any duplications. Just as a roadmap would help guide you on a trip, your editorial calendar shows you where you've been and where you're going. Getting into the habit of using an editorial calendar can take time, but it's well worth the effort.

Your Monthly Editorial Plan

The Monthly Editorial Plan helps bridge the gap between your daily tasks and your bigger goals. Refer to your Monthly Editorial Plan pages we set up in Chapter 4. This should include your master plan broken down into four weeks. This will prompt you to list out everything you want to accomplish each week during the month. You'll then figure out the smaller steps to get those big tasks accomplished and place them in the daily breakdown.

After you've brainstormed, you'll fit your content into an editorial calendar and choose your topics at least one month in advance. For example, cover the themes of your blog in any given month. Make sure you plan for seasonal articles. Let's say you decide to write a new article that you'll publish every Tuesday and to repost an older article every Thursday. You'll place those tasks in each week of the Monthly Editorial Plan. This will become your Weekly Editorial Calendar.

You'll want to plan the workflow for each type of content. List the status of each piece of the workflow under each type of content.

For example:

Weekly Entries:

    X   Article headline

    <   Needs editing

    •   Graphics complete

    X Call to action

    •   Ready for publishing

Look at any events that are important to your niche or business. Work backward and identify what content pieces you need to create in order to prime your audience for those events.

Refer to your weekly entries to break your monthly tasks down into daily schedules, such as a basic schedule for creating content and sharing on social media. It's important to take into account the time required to complete the tasks. You'll need to answer questions such as:

• Will you need to do some research?

• How long is the blog post and how long will it take to write it?

• Do you need to create any graphics?

• Will you be recording a video?

• Will you need to interview people?

Break each of the tasks down into smaller tasks and place them on your Daily Log. For example, if you need to interview someone, set aside the time it will take to contact potential people. Then set aside time to conduct the interview.

You may want to create a key to organize and visualize these tasks, such as a red dot for Pinterest, a dark blue dot for Facebook, and a green "N" for new blog post.

Make sure to project the time needed to complete your tasks in time for the deadline such as writing articles, creating graphics, taking pictures, etc. Refer back to your weekly entries to keep track of the tasks you need to complete in the next week. You'll need to identify the tasks to be completed to meet the deadlines of the upcoming week.

Here are some examples:

Daily Entries:

• Finish locating pictures for this month's new article

• Write subject line for this week's email to current subscribers.

• Create Pinterest graphic for this week

Let's say every Tuesday and Thursday, you share a new blog post. On Saturdays, you share an article from a blog you follow. On Fridays, you share a video on your Facebook page. On Sundays, you'll select the specific topics you'll be covering on your different social media accounts. Write each of these tasks in your Daily Logs. Remember to take into account that some social media will take more time than others. Instagram or Pinterest posts would obviously take more time and effort to plan than Twitter.

Keep in mind most of your planning will happen in your Daily Logs. You could compare this to a daily To Do List. I know this is not a new concept, but the point here is to use it effectively. It's so helpful to have all of your tasks in one journal with a way to track the status of when you'll complete it. You have a detailed log that you can reference at any time. For example, you can see exactly what day you sent a certain email.

You'll also know which day you didn't complete a task and where the task was moved to. Having it all in one location makes it easy to use each day.

If you're familiar with the habit of time blocking, your Daily Log is the place where this happens. If you've never heard of time blocking, it's simply another way to make sure you're making the most of your time each day. It also prevents you from trying to do too many things at once, which can make you less efficient. Here's how it works: Once you've completed your Daily Log, take a look at all the tasks you have written down. Then you'll prioritize what's on the list, ranking the items from what's most important to complete that day, to the least pressing task. Next, estimate how long it should take to finish each task. You want to make sure you set aside a realistic amount of time to accomplish your tasks. Then you'll schedule the time in your day for each of the tasks, so you'll know exactly when to stop and start each task. It's important to be realistic about each time block. If you have a large project that you know will take longer than three hours to complete, break the project down into smaller chunks of time. You want to avoid being too general with your time blocks, so that you know exactly what you to accomplish by the end of that time period. For example, you could further break down the task, "research article topic" into "conduct interviews" and "read expert survey".

One of the keys to time blocking is to make sure you don't do anything else except the scheduled task. If you're in the habit of multi-tasking, this could be a challenge for you. Research shows that multi-tasking is not the most efficient way to finish work. During the time you set aside, put away any distractions and make sure you workspace is prepared. Close all extraneous browser tabs, place your phone in a place where it will not distract you, close your social media, and do not check email until the time block is over. It can be helpful to set a timer during that time period, so that you know exactly when to start and stop that task.

While you may feel that this type of structure could stifle creativity, it's actually quite freeing. When you have time set aside that you can dedicate to deep creative work, you'll feel less stress which will make you more creative. You'll also be more consistent in spending time on creative work. Time blocking can be difficult for some people to get used to, but once you get into the habit, you'll find that you're accomplishing more in less time. You'll feel more productive and accomplished, and you'll reduce feelings of being overwhelmed by the tasks of the day.

Monthly Performance Tracker

All content needs to start with a goal. How are you going to measure its success? Is it with traffic? New subscribers? Email signups? Free Trial signups? App downloads? Conversions? Social shares? Video views? Podcast downloads? Sales? Income? Understanding the goal of each piece of content you create will guide your other decisions as you develop your content plan.

Each month, set aside an area in your monthly plan that tracks the previous month's numbers. As best you can, determine what worked and what did not work with your content so you can make adjustments. Then set goals for the new month, looking specifically at what you are measuring. For example, log into each of your social media accounts and note the number of followers. Do the same with page views and unique visitors with information from Google Analytics. This will help you see a general overview of how everything is growing, which is important in determining your next steps.

You can use an area at the bottom of your Monthly Editorial Plan to do this. Simply list the stats you want to track each month and record the results in your journal. At the end of the year, this will be a useful tool when planning for the following year. In *The One Year Content Strategy Workbook*, you'll find a "Stats Tracker" line on the bottom of each month's Editorial Plan.

Chapter 7

Content Purposes

Do you spend extra time trying to figure out exactly how you're going to write a piece of content? Do you find yourself jumping from one purpose to another without a clear end goal for your article? Your content planner can help you plan your writing time but it can also help you with how you're actually going to write it.

When thinking about the type of content to create always have your audience persona in mind. You'll want to make sure you're reaching your audience in one of these five ways:

Purpose # 1 - Attention Grabbing

You're getting their attention and educating them about a problem your product or service solves.

The type of content you create for this purpose must...

Bring attention to the problem. It needs to highlight the pain points that exist. Don't simply list the benefits. You must evoke feelings they understand before they'll listen to you. What are they going through?

Here are some examples:

• "8 Reasons Why Your Teen Never Listens To You"

• "Why Your High School Student's GPA Sucks and What To Do About It"

Purpose #2 - Trust Building

You're gaining their interest and earning their trust. You teach them more about how to solve the problem. They still have a lot of questions.

The type of content you create for this purpose must...

Maintain their interest and answer more questions. It also needs to solidify their trust in you. They're becoming more educated about the problem, but they have more questions you need to answer.

Here are a few examples:

- "The Lazy Student's Guide to Straight A's"

- "A Skill Every High School Student Should Have and Why"

Purpose #3 - Loyalty Building

You want to build their loyalty so that when they're ready to buy, they buy from you. They are aware of the problem, and they know that your product or service can solve it.

The type of content you create for this purpose must...

Tell a story that brings your message home and helps them relate to the solution. Your message must instill a desire for your product or service. Share case studies of how it solved the problem for one your clients, or even for yourself. Describe the before and after experience.

Here is an example:

"5 Questions You Should Ask Your College Counselor"

Explain why they need to consider these questions and then highlight how your product or service can help address these questions.

Purpose #4 - Action Inducing

They're ready to buy, but they need some encouragement or incentive to take action. They may have a few lingering questions.

The type of content you create for this purpose must…

Reassure them that your product or service is the right solution for them. Highlight the benefits in a way that inspires action. You can do this in the following ways:

- Share "Frequently Asked Questions" and showcase the solutions in the answers.

- Conduct a "Question and Answer" webinar.

- Respond to questions posted on social media, blog comments and emails in a timely manner.

Purpose #5 - Tribe Building

They've purchased from you and are ready for more guidance.

The type of content you create for this purpose must…

Guide them down the path to learn more about how all of your products and services can help them. You need to create strategic content that highlights related problems. Here are some examples:

- "Why It's So Difficult to Create New Habits"

- "The High Cost of Not Taking An SAT Prep Course"

This goes back to understanding your customer persona and valuing the relationship over the sale. When you take the time to nurture people who come in, they will keep listening to you. By showing you're the right person for them, they're far more likely to keep buying from you.

How do you incorporate these different content purposes into your planner? Assign a color code for the purpose of your content.

For example, if it's Attention Grabbing, label it with a red arrow. If it's Trust Building, label it with a blue arrow. If it's Action Inducing, label it with an orange arrow.

That way when you look at your Content List, you'll know the specific purpose for that piece of content.

Chapter 8

How To Find Topic Ideas & Write An Article

While you want to build your content around your brand and its purpose, it can be difficult to come up with new and interesting ideas. One of the best ways to do this effectively and efficiently is to have a formula to follow. By approaching your tasks the same way every time, you'll become skilled at finding topic ideas and writing consistently. You can use your planner to implement a content writing formula. Here are the steps:

Step 1: Collect Ideas - Walk In Your Persona's Shoes

Your writing must resonate with your audience so they trust you as their go-to source. You want to care about the same things they care about. That's why it's so important to create your audience persona. You want to write directly to that person, not to a general group of people. To do this you're going to need some inspiration. Read articles and books, watch documentaries - consume information the same way your persona would.

As you do this, look at every piece of content you encounter through the lens of your unique brand perspective. How does it relate to your mission statement? How does it fit with your brand identity? How can you fuse this topic with your perspective? When your writing is unique to you and your brand perspective it will stand out.

There are also several useful free tools you can use to find topics:

Hubspot's Blog Idea Generator - This tool gives you literally idea upon idea of topics to cover. Simply type in the terms you're interested in writing about, and it will provide you with a week's worth of relevant blog post titles.

Buzzsumo - Want to know what topics are more likely to perform well? Plug in a topic or domain, and it will tell you the most shared content for that subject.

Answer The Public - This site identifies potential content ideas using different variations of your keywords. Enter your terms, and it provides you ideas displayed in a mind map type diagram.

Here are some other ideas on how to research topics:

Look for research studies on a given topic and pick a side topic from the original study's conclusions. What other stories are within the results of the research?

Conduct your own original research study. According to Content Marketing Institute, original research is one of the best ways to gain the attention of your audience.

Step 2: Organize and Curate Topic Ideas

While you won't use every idea you come across, you'll want to organize your topics in a way that helps you determine if you should explore a topic further. You can use Evernote to clip articles from the web and save them. There are some other useful tools to keep track of topics as you come across them. Feedly organizes your online article subscriptions in one location. Similarly, Pocket makes it easy to collect and save online content across the web that you may want to refer to later.

Group By Competitiveness

When researching topic ideas, make sure you select subjects you can compete in. By doing a quick Google search, you can determine if a question has already been answered effectively. If you find several recent articles on the subject, then it's probably too competitive for your article to be discovered. That's when you do more research to hone in on different variations to find a topic that is less crowded.

For example, if you find there are only two articles that are about a year old, your newer article could have an advantage.

Curate Topic Ideas In Your Journal

Once you've grouped your ideas, organize your top ideas and transfer them to your journal in your Content Ideas collection. When going through this process, you'll end up with a lot of ideas that you'll need to sort through. Your planner will help you curate these ideas and help you get more selective about the topics you decide to write about. Make sure the topic will resonate with your audience so they read it and share it. It needs to be the best quality content that is relevant to your blog or brand. You only want to pick the best ideas to write about. Don't create content just to create content. Stick with your mission and brand identity.

Once you've determined your topics, you'll add them to your Editorial Calendar pages so you can begin writing and publishing them.

Step 3: Write Your Article

Almost all articles are written in the format listed below - no matter the length. By following this template, you can consistently build well written articles.

Article Format

Headline - Must be attention getting and clearly say what the article is about. It needs to let the reader know what's in the article before they click on it. It must make someone who is scanning stop and read the article. Using emotion and urgency will help get people interested. A good rule of thumb is to put the most important words in the first three words of the headline.

Introductory paragraph (2-4 sentences) - Includes an anecdote (a personal story that relates to the subject), or a nut graph (summarizes the essence of the story and puts it in context).

The purpose of the introductory paragraph is to grab readers with how the article pertains to them. It tells them why they should keep reading. It must be brief and interesting.

Transition to body (1-2 sentences)

Support point (3-4 sentences)

Support point (3-4 sentences)

Support point (3-4 sentences)

Closing paragraph (2-4 sentences)

Closing sentence (1 impactful sentence) - The purpose of the closing sentence is to tell readers why the article will help them, why it matters to them and why they should share it. It's your final opportunity leave them with a lasting impression. It must impact them in a way that they would want to talk about it. It makes a statement and shows them why it matters.

Step 4: Revise Your Article

Step away from the first draft of the article and edit it later with fresh eyes. When you go back to the article to revise it, begin editing out anything that is not absolutely necessary to the article. Narrow it down to its essence. Make sure it clearly follows the template above and it flows well between each section. Finally, read the article aloud and ask yourself or someone else these questions:

Is the focus of the article clear? What is the main point? If this is not clear, you need to revise the article to make sure that your main point is obvious throughout.

Does it sound natural? Does it sound conversational? If it sounds too forced or formal, readers will not connect with it. If it sounds forced, take a look at your transitions between sentences and paragraphs.

Do your thoughts transition logically from one point to the next point? Are there large gaps, leaving the reader to fill in the gaps? Are there too many words trying to make a simple point? If so, cut out unnecessary words. Be as concise and as clear as possible.

What is the mood or slant of your article? Is it humorous? Does it take a stand on something? Does it tell a story? The slant is what sets your article apart.

Chapter 9

SEO Best Practices For Your Blog Posts

One of the most important practices in SEO is remember to write for humans. Google rewards relevant content that provides people answers to what they're looking for. That's why staying in alignment with your audience persona is so important. Make sure you're not filling your content with words just to get the attention of search engines. Think about getting the attention of humans. Good results come to those who care about their audience.

Keyword Research

If you think of the internet as the freeway your audience is traveling on, then keywords are the freeway exits that lead to you. If you're new to SEO, keywords are the best place to start. Keywords help your website attract people who are looking for what you offer.

Keyword research helps you learn what those people are searching for and what they want to know. When you write about those same topics, they can find you. That's why it's important to do your keyword research before you start writing. It will also help you discover future content ideas. If you know your keyword before you start writing, you can include it naturally within your blog post or article.

Here's how to do some simple keyword research using Google AdWords:

- Sign up for a free Google AdWords account

- When you login, go to the "Campaigns" tab and locate the Keyword Planner tool

- Click on "Get search volume and data trends"

- Enter some keyword ideas into the box, one per line

- Click on "Get search volume"

The results will show you how many people are searching for the terms you entered. You can keep doing this as more terms come to mind. You can then determine which keywords have the most people searching and are most appropriate for your brand and topic.

To keep it real, use variations of your keyword. Use your main keyword in the recommended areas, but then change it up. Above all, you don't want your writing to sound repetitive, redundant or unnatural.

Keyword Placement

Once you've identified your keywords. It's important to put them in the right places in your blog posts. Here is where they need to go:

- Blog Post Title

- Post URL

- At least one heading within your article

- Image title

- Image ALT description

- Pinterest pin description

Keyword Density

The rule of thumb is to aim to use your keyword about 1.5% of the number of words in your post. Simply divide the number of times you used the keyword by the total number of words in your post. You can also use the Keyword Density Analyzer tool at SEObook.com to figure this out.

Blog Post Format

It's important to format your blog posts so that readers can easily skim your page. This is also important for SEO purposes. The following is the recommended way to format blog posts:

- Clear, actionable title

- Short paragraphs (2-3 sentences at the most)

- Headings, images and white space that break up text

- Keyword included a few times within the post

- Keyword once in a heading

- Font size 14-16 pt

- Use callout boxes and bold text for important points

- Applicable, attractive images

Length of Article

It's widely known that Google favors long content over short content. Your article should be between 500-1000 words for Google to index it. That said, you can't go wrong with longer posts. However - quality is always priority one. According to Marccx Media, there is no one-size-fits-all approach to content length. They say that while some sites see significant traffic with just a few hundred word posts, others create content with over 5,000 words to rank well.

They recommend that you determine your content length based on these factors:

Where you share your content - Shorter content performs better on social media.

Your industry - Ultra competitive industries demand longer content.

Your target audience - Younger audiences respond more favorably to shorter content, while longer content will rank better with older audiences over age forty.

Your authority - If you have established credibility in your niche, you can do well with shorter content.

That said, don't get distracted and overly focused on the length of your content. Think about why Google might favor longer content. The reason? It tends to provide more value to the reader. That's what it's all about. That's what makes your site rank well. Consistent value that readers can rely on. Google wants to make sure people get useful and interesting information. Don't make it too light, but don't make it long and rambling.

Create "Sub-Topic" Content

Instead of focusing on over saturated topics, look for sub-topics that are easier to compete in. The key is to identify potential sub-topics early and build authority within that topic. Look for new and emerging areas of interest that are related to your niche before they become saturated with content. The earlier you spot the opportunity, the more time you have to establish yourself as an authority on that topic. Create quality content that answers the emerging questions, and you'll be one step ahead of your competition.

If you can connect with buyers early in the decision making process, they can get to know you before it's time to make a decision. When you cover information that's just outside your niche but still related, you can teach your audience about topics they're interested in, making them more likely to read and click through your articles. Research shows that people are 2-3 times more likely to click through your content when they're familiar with you and your brand. They're also 2-3 times more likely to buy from you.

Planting Seeds - Growing Flowers and Weeds

We know that quality content matters, but quantity also matters. Here's why: the more content you produce, the higher your chances of reaching your audience with articles that really speak to them. Think of each piece of content as starting out as a seed. The more seeds you scatter, the greater your chances of growing a flower - but remember, you'll also grow some weeds.

Flowers will have higher click through rates and more time spent on the page. They increase your brand affinity.

The more content you write, the more likely you'll be to grow a flower, and the more you'll increase your brand affinity. In contrast, weeds will have lower click through rates and low engagement. Don't be discouraged by weeds. They're not a failure - just a natural byproduct of your efforts. Weeds happen.

By scrutinizing your your content and evaluating whether it's a flower or a weed, you can decide what content to expand on and replicate into more content. You'll learn when to keep focusing on a certain topic and when to move on. If you have a flower, maximize its value. Infographics, follow-up stories, social media ads, webinars - use all that firepower to extract the maximum value from that topic. By having a frequent volume of blog posts, you'll discover what content is mediocre and what content could bloom into a flower. You're scattering seeds to grow a beautiful flower.

Chapter 10

Where to Share Your Content

According to Search Engine Journal, there are several alternative places to share your content other than the obvious choices of Facebook and Twitter. They're less competitive, yet they still have a lot of traffic, giving you have a better chance of standing out.

Here are some alternative places across the web to share your content:

Slideshare - Turn your writing into a quality powerpoint slideshow or video and share it as a presentation.

Visual.ly - Convert your content into an infographic or other visual graphic and share it in the community there.

LinkedIn Groups - Target your messaging within specific groups and reach beyond your LinkedIn connections. A word of caution - don't spam! Make sure your content is relevant to the group and that it welcomes sharing content.

Instagram - Similar to Pinterest, this visual social sharing site is popular with the younger demographic.

Triberr - Targeted "tribes" within this network allow you to share each other's content so you can build relationships with other content creators and earn traffic.

StumbleUpon - Add your content to this social network where users can browse random web pages. If it is well liked, it will be more likely to appear in the random search rotation.

BizSugar - If your audience is small business related, you can share small business news and tips, helping you increase your online presence.

Scoop It - Create your own curated content page here to create and grow your online presence.

BlogEngage - This blog sharing website allows you to post on a wide variety of topics to help build your audience.

Your Social Media Strategy

Where does your target audience seem to be the most active? Is one channel more popular within that demographic? Different social networks may attract different demographics who may all be part of your target market. Your target audience may want to see different content depending on the channel. You can look up who you're reaching in your different social media channels by looking at the analytics for each of your social media accounts. By learning more about who you're reaching on each channel you can adjust your content to provide what they want to see.

When thinking about your social media strategy, it's important to stay informed on on current trends in the world of social media and content marketing. Algorithms change and social sharing habits change. When you build a solid reputation for authoritative, original content, you're less likely to fall victim to the changes that are outside your control. Also, make sure that anything you share with your audience is well researched from a trusted source.

People will tend to share authoritative, reference content that never becomes outdated. Known as "evergreen" content, it consistently gains links and shares over time. We'll discuss more on how to build evergreen content in Chapter 12. As you determine who is following you on social media, write a short paragraph in your Promotional Channels page that describes what content you share and why it's important to your followers. For example, "XYZ Company provides the most actionable marketing advice on the web. This content is important to our audience because they want to learn how to work more effectively."

Chapter 11

Word Lists

When we're moved, intrigued or challenged immediately by an article, it's not an accident. Successful writers strategically choose their words when trying to elicit a specific response from the reader. In this chapter, we'll share some handy words to help you write better for specific purposes. By using these words at the right time, you'll automatically be a better writer. Choose from these lists and add them to your "List of Power Words" page in your planner.

Power Words For Headlines

free, sale, new, professional, guaranteed, special, tested, improved, immediately, limited, simplistic, powerful, big, popular, exclusive, valuable, how to, endorsed, unlimited, discount, fundamentals, underpriced, suddenly, perspective, launching, skill, reduced, better, shrewd, enormous, spotlight, useful, survival, largest, colossal, now, unlock, fortune, authentic, announcing, huge, gift, introducing, practical, focus, wanted, absolutely, lowest, interesting, challenge, lifetime, highest, expert, advice, the truth about, compare, colorful, adorable, ultimate, willpower, attractive, easily, approved, competitive, full, mammoth, innovative, it's here, just arrived, sure, fire, soar, beautiful, crammed, growth, promising, astonishing, imagination, greatest, high-tech, latest, important, urgent, amazing, exciting, portfolio, revealing, sensational, excellent, remarkable, obsession, surging, revisited, unique, bargain, hurry, daring, pioneering, destiny, unsurpassed, genuine, informative, mainstream, complete, last chance, exploit, quality, gigantic, love, lavishly, reliable, terrific, breakthrough, emerging, profitable, sampler, noted, luxury, unconditional, timely, bonanza, security, refundable, quickly, revolutionary, miracle, magic, proven, reward, weird, surprise, delighted, confidential, sizable, wonderful, delivered, secrets, scarce, alert, famous, strong, unusual, outstanding, energy, instructive, liberal, rare, edge, superior, unparalleled, fascinating, compromise, odd, bottom line, zinger, simplified, tremendous, helpful, special, technology, selected, sturdy, wealth, successful, opportunities, last minute, monumental, startling, quick, easy, direct, simple, strange, value, insider, download

Power Words of Encouragement

Triumph, Bravery, Mind-blowing, Magical, Sensational, Fearless, Courage, Hope,

Power Words That Evoke Curiosity

Unauthorized, What they don't want you to know, Off limits, Limited Access, Elite, Behind the Scenes, Secret, Banned, Black market, Insider, Controversial, Concealed, Locked Away, Cover up, Confidential, Limited Edition, Insiders Only, Forbidden

Power Words for Money

Skyrocket, Freebie, Giveaway, BOGO, Rewards, Discount, Free, Jackpot, Markdown, Savings, Rock Bottom, Barely Used, Employee Discount, Insider Discount, Special, Pennies, Dollar, Cheap, Slashed, Limited Time, One Time Only, Just for Loyal Customers, Inexpensive, Gift, Fortune, Advantage, Triple, Double, Prize

David Ogilvy's List of Most Influential Words

Suddenly, Now, Announcing, Introducing, Improvement, Amazing, Sensational, Remarkable, Revolutionary, Startling, Miracle, Magic, Offer, Quick, Easy, Wanted, Challenge, Compare, Bargain, Hurry

Words That Convey Trust

anonymous, authentic, backed, best-selling, cancel anytime, certified, endorsed, guaranteed, ironclad, lifetime, money back, no obligation, no questions asked, no risk, no strings attached, official, privacy, protected, proven, recession-proof, refund, research, results, secure, tested, try before you buy, verify, unconditional

Chapter 12

How To Build A Bank Of Evergreen Content

As we discussed in the beginning of this book, it can be a struggle to find topic ideas. The strategies in this book provide a formula to follow to keep you from falling into the trap of chasing the latest trend or coming up with topics on the fly.

With everything we've covered, you might still be wondering how to sustain your content over time. One of the best ways to have an endless supply of useful content is to build a bank of evergreen topic ideas. Evergreen content is timeless. It remains relevant whatever the season, week month or year. It's highly valuable because your audience will always find it interesting no matter when they read it. Because of it's high value, it helps you rank well with search engines over time.

When you deposit regularly to your bank of evergreen content, you'll have an asset to draw from. You can you maximize its value because it continues to generate traffic long after it's first published, and you can repurpose it and share it on social media any time.

Because you've taken the time to create an audience persona, it should help you identify evergreen content your audience would find interesting.

Here are some ideas to help you get started in creating a bank of evergreen content:

- Transform a topic you've already written about by writing from another view. For example, if you wrote an article on the best practices for a subject, so another article on the do's and don'ts.

- Research topics your competitors have written about and think of new angle to explore on the subject.

- Are there frequently asked questions from your customers? Convert their questions and the answers into an article.

- Do you have specific industry advice or explanations to offer?

- Can you clarify some common industry misconceptions?

Here are some ideas for creating evergreen content:

- Lists, Checklists

- Top Tips

- How-To Guides

- Product Reviews

- Historical Articles

- Informational Articles

- Resource Lists

- Glossaries of Terms

- Testimonials

- Year In Review Summaries

- Interviews

- Case Studies

- Success Stories

When you create evergreen content, you're ensuring that you'll always have something to share. Keep in mind, it doesn't always have to be in the form of an article. Your evergreen content can also be in an infographic, picture or video.

Make sure all of your evergreen content includes the following:

A Hook - to get the audience's attention

In Depth Information - Your audience needs to learn as much as possible on the subject. Use reliable sources to establish trust and an authority.

Updated Information - If something changes with the nature of your content, make sure you update to reflect the most current information. This will keep your content ranking well with search engines.

While you also want to include on-trend, or seasonal content in your strategy, producing evergreen content can differentiate you from your competition and establish you as an authority in your niche. That's why you must make sure it truly adds value to your audience, solves a problem or answers a question.

By including both on-trend and evergreen content, you'll build a bank of valuable content that will drive leads and provide value to your audience for years to come.

Appendix

Tools & Resources for Content Writers

Researching Content Ideas

- Buzz Sumo

- Answer The Public

- Scrapbook.com

- Blog Title Generator by SEOpressor.com

Keyword Research

- LSI Keyword Generator Tool

- Keyword Finder

- Keyword Revealer

- Keywordtool.io

Headline Writing

- Hubspot Blog Topic Generator

- CoSchedule Headline Analyzer

- Inbound Blog Headline Generator

- AMI Headline Analyzer

Organization/Workflow

- **Pocket** - This tool allows you to read and categorize articles that you would like to save for later and follow your trusted sources of information all in one place.

- **Feedly** - This feed reader works similar to Pocket and helps you organize blogs and other articles in one location. You can also easily share the stories you read with others.

- **Airtable** - This collaboration tool helps you organize information and manage projects.

- **Trello** - This web based project management app keeps track of everything. It works well for managing multiple projects and collaborating with others. It's simple, yet powerful.

- **OneTab** - If you're like me, you often have many tabs open on your browser at the same time, and this really slows down your computer's performance. OneTab is a free Chrome extension that organizes all of your open tabs into a single list of links, which is less taxing on your computer's memory and bandwidth. Once you organize everything into OneTab, you'll have all your research organized in one place. This is one of my personal favorites.

Proofreading/Editing

- **Hemingway** - If you want help making your writing bold and clear, this app is for you. It highlights lengthy, awkward sentences, passive voice, overused words and more. It's a standalone program that costs $20.

- **Grammarly** - A free editing app that makes sure your writing is clear, mistake-free and effective. You can also upgrade to the premium version for more advanced writing help.

- **SlickWrite** - A free app that checks your writing for grammar errors and potential style mistakes.

- **ProWriting Aid** - This free online editing tool will flag errors, recommend style improvements and help you find the right words. It will run proofreading reports for plagiarism, corporate wording, overused words and many more. You can also set up your own customized reports such as a brand style check report.

-

Word Choice

- OneLook Dictionary & Thesaurus

- The Idioms

- Words to Use

- Alliteration.me

- RhymeZone.com

Social Sharing

- **CrowdTangle** - This free Chrome extension allows you to see who shares your content, allowing you to reach out to them to build relationships. When you click the icon in your browser bar, a menu will appear with the names of everyone who shared that page. You can then click the social media icon next to the person's name to open the post where they shared your content. You'll also see an Interactions column where you can find people who have shared your page multiple times.

On Page SEO

- Moz - One of the most trusted resources for all things SEO

Recommended Books

- *The Elements of Style*, William Strunk

- *Steal Like An Artist*, Austin Kleon

- *On Writing Well*, William Zinger

Digital Apps To Use For Journaling

- Evernote

- Goodnotes

- Notability

Afterword

Writing content and constantly coming up with ideas on what to write about can be overwhelming. Getting your message out in a way that leads to more traffic and more sales is challenging in the noisy world we live in. *What Is Content Strategy?* was created to help reduce some of this stress by giving you a formula to follow - to help make the task a little less overwhelming and to help you grow your business.

Thank You!

If you feel this book was helpful and could benefit others, I have a favor to ask of you. Would you please leave a review on Amazon? I would greatly appreciate it.

About The Author

Sandra Shillington is a copywriter and a certified content marketer. She helps businesses craft the perfect message - whether it's web content, blog posts, ebooks, authority guides or training courses. Sandra has a BS in Business Administration from Pepperdine University.

References

"Back to SEO Basics: Ideal Content Length for SEO?" Marcxx Media. October 19, 2015. Web. January 30, 2018.

"Developing A Content Marketing Strategy." Content Marketing Institute. Web. January 26, 2018.

Dooley, Roger. "Paper Beats Digital In Many Ways, According To Neuroscience." Forbes. September 16, 2015. Web. February 12, 2018.

Lee, Kevan. "189 Power Words That Convert: Write Copy That Gets Your Customer's Attention Every Time." BufferSocial. July 2, 2014. Web. February 1, 2018.

Morrow, Jon. "317 Power Words That Will Instantly Make You A Better Writer." Smartblogger. October 19, 2017. Web. January 20, 2018.

Newport, Cal. "Deep Habits: The Importance of Planning Every Minute of Your Workday." CalNewport.com. December 21, 2013. Web. March 1, 2018.

Patel, Sujan. "15 Places You Should Be Sharing Your Blog Posts (Other Than Facebook or Twitter)." Search Engine Journal. April 14, 2015. Web. January 30, 2018.

Rayson, Steve. "Content Trends Report 2018." Buzzsumo. March 2018. Web. March 1, 2018.

Rourke, Lee. "Why Creative Writing Is Better With a Pen." The Guardian. November 3, 2011. Web. February 1, 2018.

Yates, Scott. "4 Useful Tips For Creating Evergreen Content." Hubspot. Web. February 21, 2018.